The Artistry of
Bill Evans

Many thanks to CPP/Belwin, Inc. for their commitment to the artistry of my late husband, Bill Evans.

Nenette Evans

Nenette Evans

c/o TRO
11 West 19th Street
New York, NY 10011

Editors: David C. Olsen and Tom Roed
Transcriptions by Pascal Wetzel
Cover Photo by Fantasy Records

"Bill Evans...A Remembrance"
by Charles Blancq

Few musicians in the history of jazz have had as great an impact on its structure and syntax as the late jazz pianist Bill Evans. From the beginning of his career in the mid-1950s to his untimely death in the fall of 1980, Evans did more to enrich the vocabulary of the jazz pianist and to ensure the continuation of the jazz rhythm trio than any other pianist of his generation.

Born William John Evans on August 16, 1929 in Plainfield, New Jersey, Evans began musical training at an early age. By the time he was thirteen, he had already augmented his piano studies with violin and flute instruction, and was apprenticing as the pianist in a local New Jersey dance band. It was here that Evans first experimented with jazz, by altering the piano part on the then popular "Tuxedo Junction," and thus discovering the potential of jazz improvisation. The desire to master his newly acquired skill continued throughout his college years at Southeastern Louisiana College, his four-year stint in the Army as a flutist and pianist in the 5th Army Band at Fort Sheridan, and his long apprenticeship (first in Chicago and later in New York), where he played and recorded with an impressive number of established jazzmen, including Jerry Wald, Tony Scott, Dick Garcia, Charlie Mingus and George Russell. But his most important and critical association was still forthcoming. In 1958, Miles Davis hired him to replace Red Garland in his recently formed sextet, and with Miles, Bill became the conceptual force on KIND OF BLUE (Columbia CS-8163) by contributing two originals to that historic album, "Blue in Green" and "Flamenco Sketches." The association with Miles helped establish Evans as an important new voice in jazz, and provided him with the acknowledgement he needed in launching his own career as a leader. Beginning in 1959, he began to devote more of his energies to the formation of his own trio -a medium that he would almost singlehandedly reform during the early 1960s.

The solo pianist, as well as the pianist who fronted rhythm trios had a long and integral role in the history of jazz, and indeed, there were many pianists who had made significant contributions to this tradition. Modest and unassuming as he was, Evans always acknowledged the contributions of these pioneering artists, and had in particular cited Art Tatum, Nat Cole, George Shearing and Bud Powell as having a long-lasting influence on him. But Evans' concept of the trio differed from that of his predecessors. In the rhythm trio before his time, the piano was the dominant instrument and the other instruments played secondary roles. Evans' approach was fundamentally different, for he envisioned a more equal dialogue between piano, bass and drums based on simultaneous improvisation. These ideas, somewhat novel for the time, eventually found fruition in the performances of his "first trio" (with bassist Scott LaFaro and drummer Paul Motian) and culminated in the celebrated Village Vanguard recordings of 1961 (now available as THE VILLAGE VANGUARD SESSIONS, Milestone 47002).

Evans' contributions as a leader of trios would in itself ensure him a place in jazz history, but more importantly, he must be regarded as one of the most innovative pianists in modern jazz. The very personal harmonic language that he perfected through his many systematic reharmonizations of standard tunes (and his own originals), has influenced an entire generation of jazz pianists. The long, lyrical melodic lines, asymmetrical phrasing and especially his light, mobile (and often rootless) chord-voicings with the characteristic whole-step or semi-tone clash in the left hand, have now entered the vocabulary of virtually every modern jazz pianist of the last twenty-five years.

He was, after all, a "total" pianist; his mastery of the piano was as complete as any pianist of his time or before, and his music was not based on any commercial motivation or an exaggeration of one particular skill. Although an extraordinary technician, his technique was never an end in itself - but was subordinated instead to an overall musical message. Thus, his performances possess an inner cohesion and continuity that place him among the finest jazz musicians of his generation.

Untouched by both the new jazz of the early 1960s and the fusion movement of the 1970s, Evans patiently followed his own musical instincts, producing a large number of recordings that were remarkable for their consistent inventiveness. Not that his work went unrecognized, he was after all the recipient of five Grammy Awards, and several nominations, but a certain misconception about Evans prevailed nevertheless: that he was a brooding romantic whose music was characterized by a uniform range of musical expression. Actually, nothing was further from the truth: Evans was in many ways the ultimate assimilator of a large variety of musical influences - a musical poet, whose language revealed an inclination for the romantic and melancholy at times, but one who was also capable of a high-powered, exuberant, swinging performance as well.

The majority of the transcriptions that follow date from the trio performances of the 1970s - a period during which Evans at times expanded his group to include guest performers such as Toots Thielemans, Larry Schneider, Harold Land, Kenny Burrell, Lee Konitz, Warne Marsh and Tom Harrell. But Evans was still first and foremost the trio performer, and it was his concept of the trio, now well defined, that permitted him to direct his creative energies towards collaborative efforts with others. In many ways this was the most fertile decade of Evans' career, for he recorded frequently, formed a long-lasting musical relationship with bassist Eddie Gomez, and made the greatest strides in the expansion of his repertoire. What the recordings from this period and these transcriptions reveal is that Evans was indeed the great romantic and lyrical player he was reputed to be, but he was also much more than that. In this, the last decade of his life, his playing took on a new vibrancy and a new challenge.

One can learn much from the music of Bill Evans: the economy of his musical statement, his highly original harmonic and melodic concept, his creative and often startling sense of rhythmic subdivision and his free-flowing sense of phrase construction. Seeing his music transcribed into notation reveals all of this and more, for Evans was a great interpreter of both his own and others' compositions, and his improvisations stand as evidence of his enduring accomplishment.

Charles Blancq
Department of Music
University of New Orleans

Emily

By
JOHNNY MERCER and
JOHNNY MANDEL

Rubato

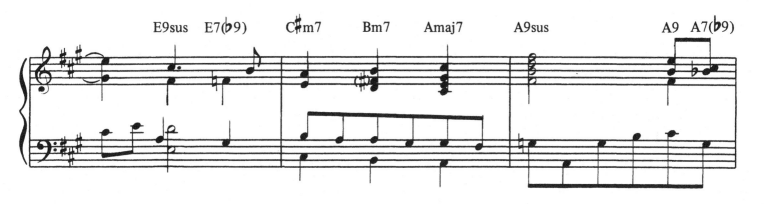

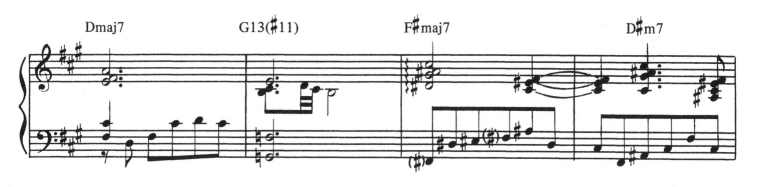

14

Alfie

By
HAL DAVID and
BURT BACHARACH

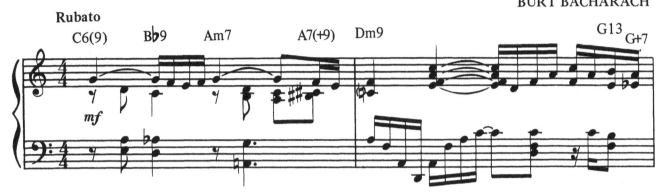

(Bass and Drums enter)

I Will Say Goodbye
(Je Vivrai Sans Toi)

By
MICHEL LEGRAND and
EDDY MARNAY

Left
to Right:

Eliot Zigmund,
Drum

Eddie Gomez,
Bass

Bill Evans,
Piano

Photo by:
Swing Journal

Left
to Right:

Bill Evans

Eddie Gomez

Photo by:
Giuseppe Pino

Left
to Right:

Bill Evans

Eddie Gomez

Photo by:
Hans Hartziem

Dolphin Dance

Music by
HERBIE HANCOCK

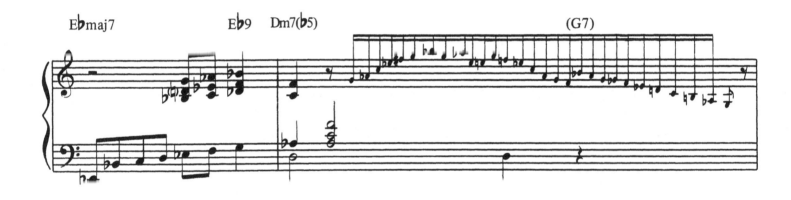

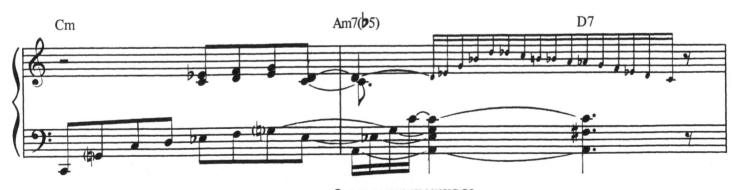

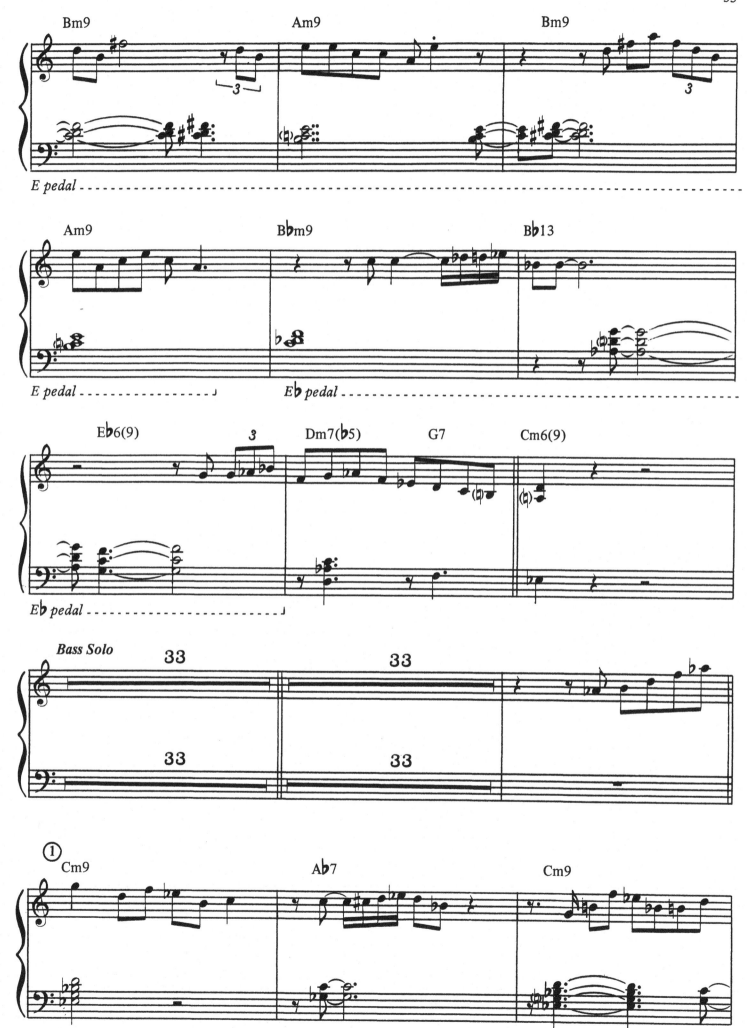

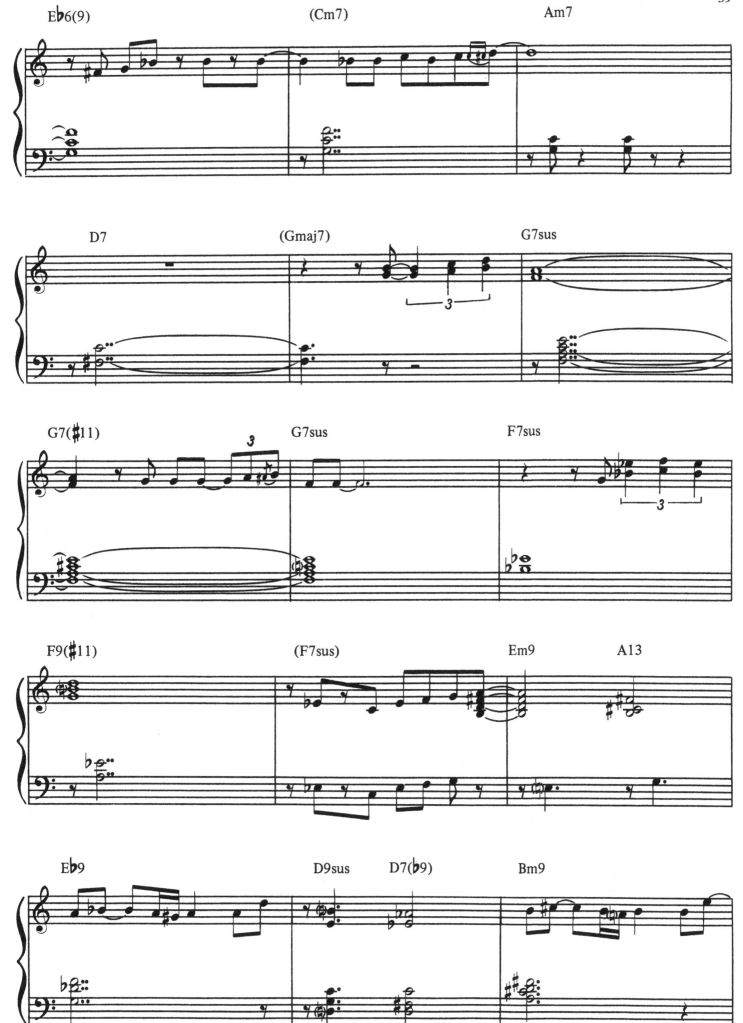

40

Never Let Me Go

Words and Music by
JAY LIVINGSTON and
RAY EVANS

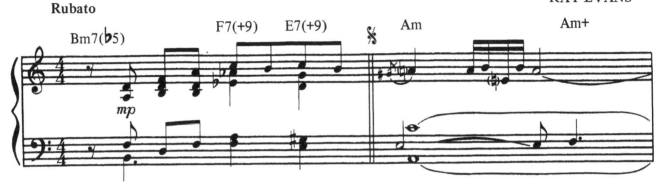

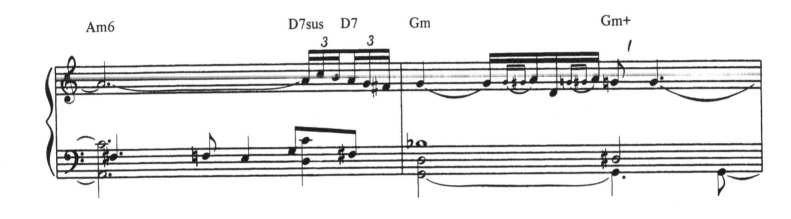

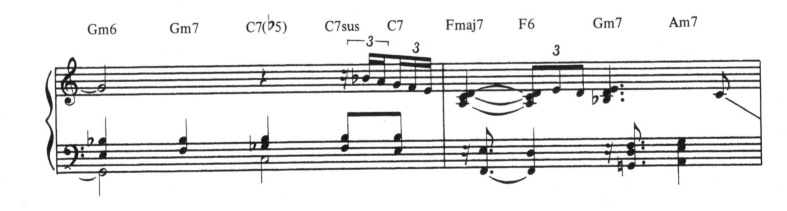

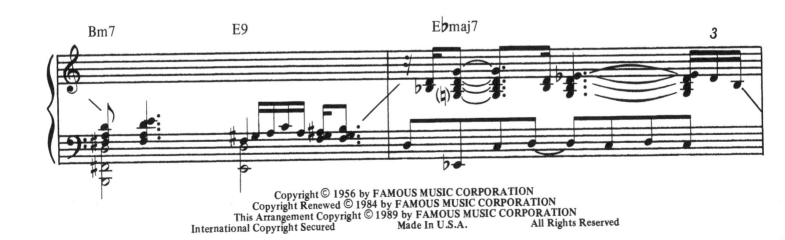

But Beautiful

By
JOHNNY BURKE and
JIMMY VAN HEUSEN

53

56

Seascape

By
JOHNNY MANDEL

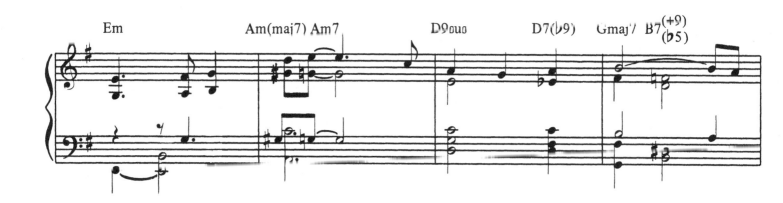

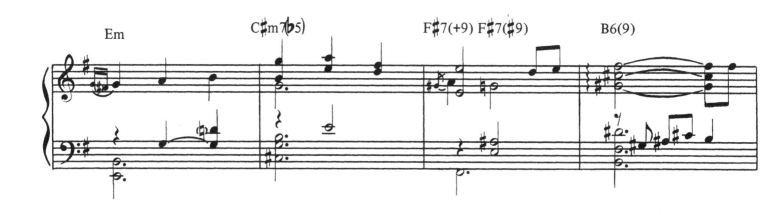

60

Piano Solo
Rubato

You Must Believe In Spring

By
MICHEL LEGRAND and
JACQUES DEMY

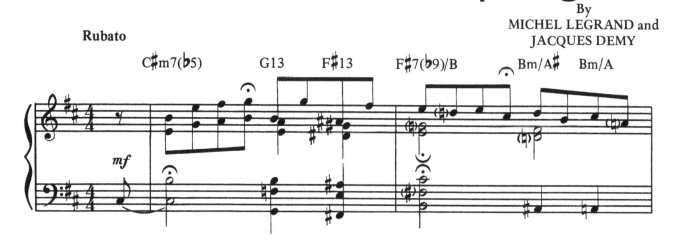

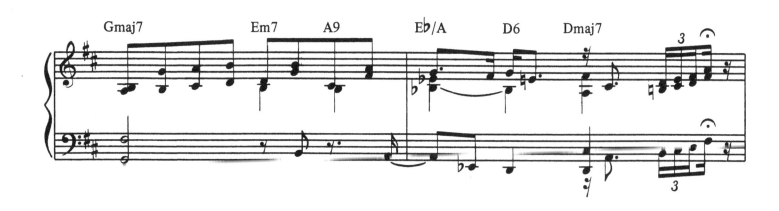

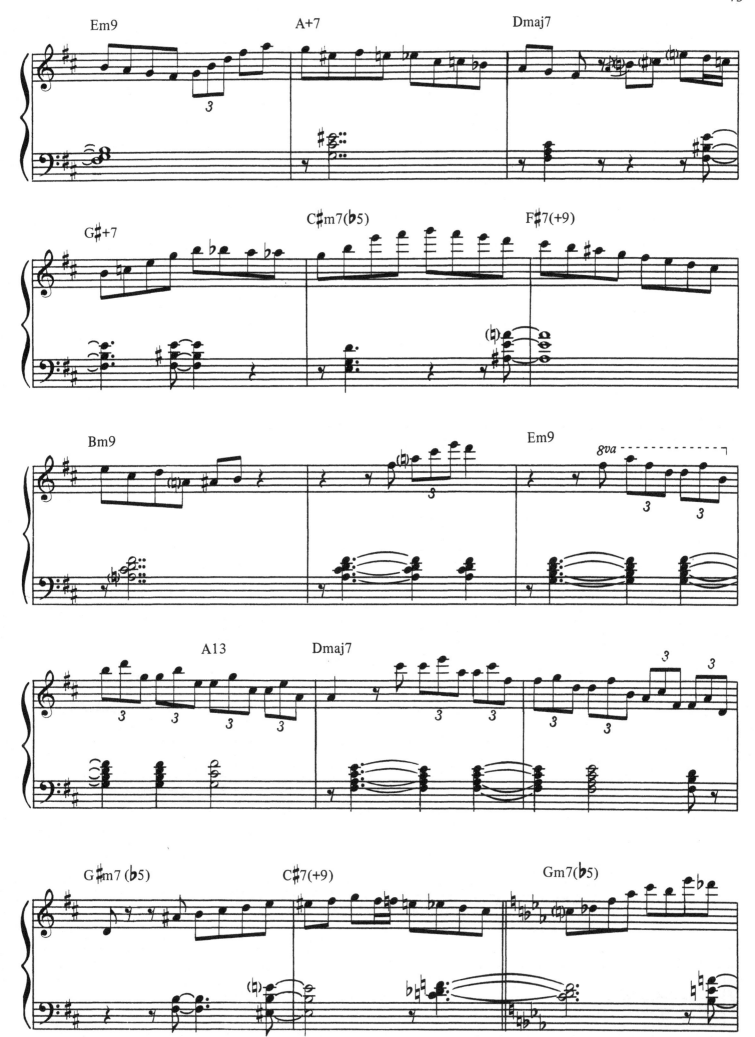

The Summer Knows
(Theme From "Summer of '42")

By
MARILYN and ALAN BERGMAN
and MICHEL LEGRAND

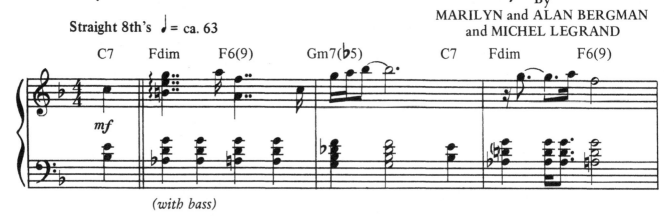

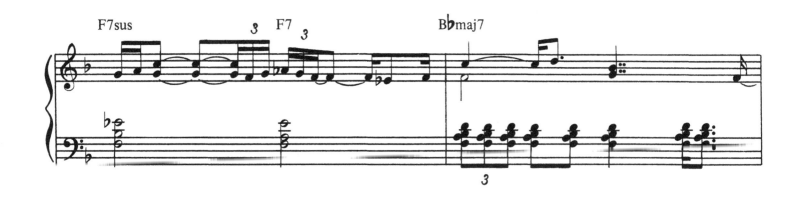

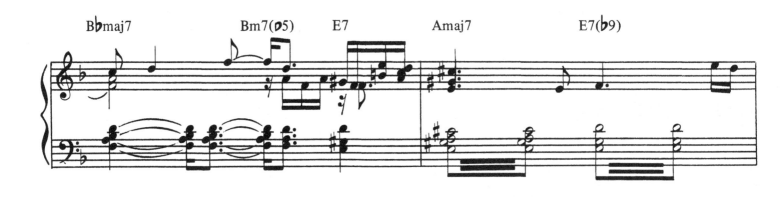

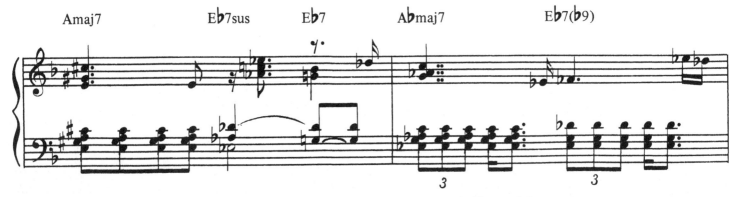

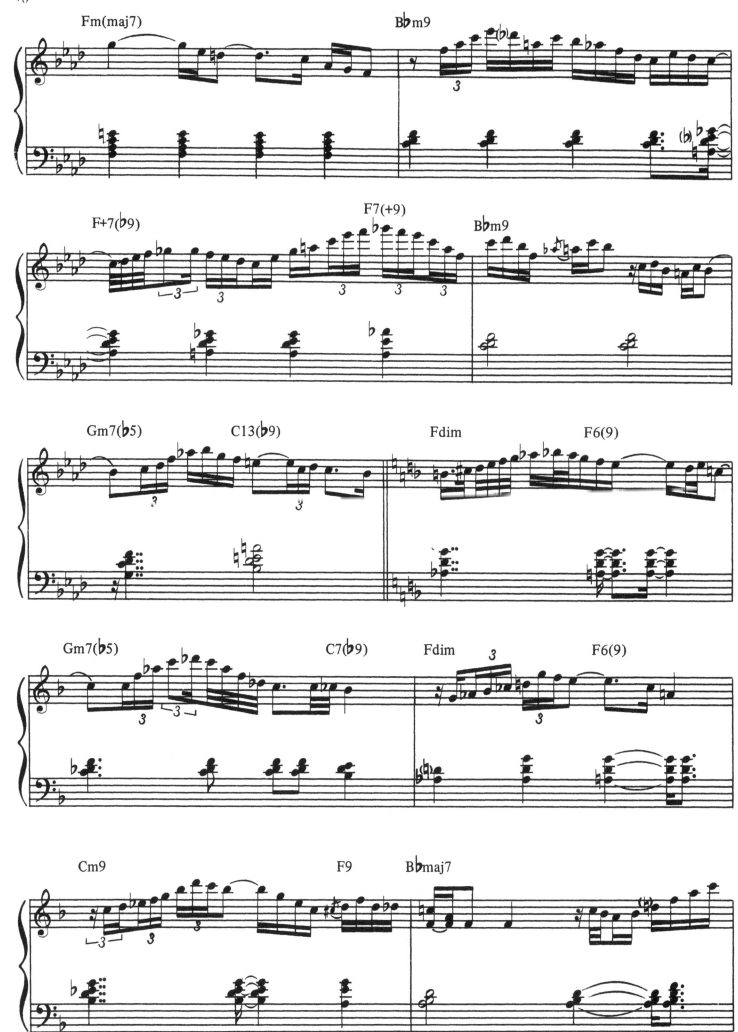

A Time For Love

By
PAUL FRANCIS WEBSTER and
JOHNNY MANDEL

Photo by: Francis Paudras